#ENTRYLEVELtweet

Taking Your Career from Classroom to Cubicle

By Heather R. Huhman
Foreword by Mark Stelzner,
Founder of JobAngels

Copyright © 2010 by Heather R. Huhman

All rights reserved. No patent liability is assumed with respect to the use of the information contained herein. Although every precaution has been taken in the preparation of this book, the publisher and author(s) assume no responsibility for errors or omissions. Neither is any liability assumed for damages resulting from the use of the information contained herein.

First Printing: February 2010

Paperback ISBN: 978-1-61699-024-4 (1-61699-024-4)

Place of Publication: Silicon Valley, California USA

Paperback Library of Congress Number: 2010920818

eBook ISBN: 978-1-61699-025-1 (1-61699-025-2)

Trademarks

All terms mentioned in this book that are known to be trademarks or service marks have been appropriately capitalized. Happy About® and its imprint, THINKaha™, cannot attest to the accuracy of this information. Use of a term in this book should not be regarded as affecting the validity of any trademark or service mark.

Warning and Disclaimer

Every effort has been made to make this book as complete and as accurate as possible, but no warranty of fitness is implied. The information provided is on an "as is" basis. The authors and the publisher shall have neither liability nor responsibility to any person or entity with respect to loss or damages arising from the information contained in this book.

Advance Praise

"'#ENTRYLEVELtweet' is straight to the point and packed with poignant success tips for college grads embarking on their first career."

Anne Brown, @*gradtogreat*, Editor, GradtoGreat.com

"'#ENTRYLEVELtweet' breaks the complexities of job search into practical, bite-sized career commandments that are spot on. Read. Do. Repeat."

Kristi Daeda, @*kristid*, Personal Marketing Strategist, Writer, and Coach at KristiDaeda.com

---

"'#ENTRYLEVELtweet' offers practical, easy-to-implement steps every job seeker should be following. This is a must-read for college students and recent grads."

Grace Kutney, @*sweetcareers*, Career Advisor, Sweet Careers Consulting

---

"It's simple. Read '#ENTRYLEVELtweet' and you'll learn how to attract attention…the right way!"

J.T. O'Donnell, @*jtodonnell*, Nationally Syndicated Career Expert, Author, and Founder of CAREEREALISM.com

"@collegegrads, read this #book if you want a quick, easy-to-read guide on how to go from a confused graduate to a confident entry-level worker."

Dan Schawbel, *@danschawbel*, Author of 'Me 2.0: Build a Powerful Brand to Achieve Career Success'

"'#ENTRYLEVELtweet' is sorely needed 4 2day's overwhelmed job seeker. Personal branding 2 developing an online strategy cover 2 cover in 15 min!"

Joshua Waldman, *@joshuawaldman*, Career Consultant and Blogger for CareerEnlightenment.net

---

"Crisp, efficient, and full of useful job hunting advice. I would recommend this to anyone looking for an entry-level job!"

Trevor Wilson, *@gradversity*, Founder, Gradversity.com

Dedication

To my husband Brett for his endless support and love during this incredible journey.

Acknowledgments

Thanks to the entire *@ComeRecommended* team for being an incredibly talented and inspiring bunch.

Thank you *@examinercom* for giving me my first real platform on which to share my knowledge and build my brand.

Special thanks to my publisher Mitchell Levy *@HappyAbout* for taking on my first book.

Why Did I Write This book?

For the most part, pending and recent graduates do not know how to search for a job.

Hiring managers expect young professionals to be job hunting experts.

There's a strong need for quick, easy-to-digest information about entry-level job searching.

I wrote '#ENTRYLEVELtweet' to fulfill that need.

Landing an entry-level job one day sooner means you're one day sooner to your dream position.

Read, share, and fulfill your dreams!

All the best!

Heather R. Huhman, *@heatherhuhman*

Taking Your Career from Classroom to Cubicle

Contents

Foreword   11

Section I
Identifying Your "Unique You"   13

Section II
Developing Your "Career Tools"   25

Section III
Networking as a Job Search Tool   69

Section IV
Applying for Internships & Entry-Level Jobs   81

Section V
Accepting & Rejecting Offers   93

Section VI

Succeeding on the Job 9

About the Author 10

Foreword by Mark Stelzner

Heather Huhman has demystified career guidance with '#ENTRYLEVELtweet.' Read it, absorb it, use it, and change your world.

Mark Stelzner, *@stelzner*

Founder and Chairman, JobAngels Founder, Inflexion Advisors

Workforce Advisory Board Member, SmartBrief

Visit him at: http://www.inflexionadvisors.com/principals.html

Taking Your Career from Classroom to Cubicle

Section 1

Identifying Your "Unique You"

Organizations want to hire employees who provide results. While you might not have much work experience, you have plenty to offer. This chapter will help you learn how to assess your personal and professional strengths.

Taking Your Career from Classroom to Cubicle

1

Many people in your life will steer you down a career path because it's one they've deemed "successful" or "practical."

2

Others, namely your parents, will "strongly encourage" you to take the first job you're offered out of college.

3

Individuals in your life love you dearly and give you advice with the best intentions. But they're probably wrong.

4

You need to choose a career that makes you happy and excited about going to work, but remember that not every day on the job will be fun.

5
Don't beat yourself up for *not* making the right choice at first—most of us don't!

6
Listen to yourself, to *your* needs and wants rather than those of the people around you.

7

There, I've said it. You're now in charge of your life's direction—your *career's* direction!

8

Take out a sheet of paper, and write down every skill, characteristic, and interest you have.

9

Perhaps you've had the fantastic ability of persuasion since you were young, or you've been playing the piano for more than a decade.

10

Make your "unique you" list as comprehensive as possible!

11

Remember those well-intentioned people who love you? Ask them to help you identify your skills, characteristics, and interests.

12

Let's examine your list and begin to organize it. There are three different types of skills: adaptive, transferable, and job-specific.

13

Adaptive skills, such as honesty and enthusiasm, describe your personality.

14

Transferable skills, such as strong writing are general and can be used in a variety of jobs.

15

Job-specific skills typically require training or experience.

16

When written out, no two people's skills, characteristics, and interests are *exactly* the same. You've just identified your "unique you."

17

Your "unique you" list is "living"—it will change often throughout your career.

Taking Your Career from Classroom to Cubicle

Section II

Developing Your "Career Tools"

What exactly do hiring managers look for when evaluating you and your application? In this chapter, you will learn how to develop your "career tools": accomplishment stories, cover letter, résumé, social networking profiles, an online portfolio, business cards, and references.

18

Even in a candidate-saturated market, there are many more (and better) ways to get in front of hiring managers than there used to be.

19

In the old days, you'd email your résumé en masse or just scour the "big three" online job boards hoping someone would see your résumé.

Taking Your Career from Classroom to Cubicle

20

Say good-bye to the old tactics and prepare for the era of Job Search 2.0.

21

Your new "career toolbox" will include more than just a cover letter and résumé.

22

You're going to need accomplishment stories, social networking profiles, an online portfolio, business cards, and references.

23

Although your career tools will change, once you have a basic understanding of how to create each one, future revisions will be easy.

24

For your accomplishment stories, make a list of ten skills (i.e., HTML) and ten characteristics (i.e., enthusiasm) you have to offer.

25

Each skill and characteristic will develop into its own story—or several stories.

26

Some questions to ask yourself about each skill: How and why did you obtain it? What makes it important to have?

27

Questions to ask yourself about each characteristic: Is there an example of a time when it came in handy? How does it set you apart?

28

You should now have several stories about each skill and characteristic from your original list of ten each.

29

While some people believe cover letters are a huge waste of time, I am certainly not one of them. I always read cover letters first.

30

Your cover letter is about what *you* can do for the *company* and why you make a good fit for both the position and the organization.

31

Cover letters are neither about your life story nor your needs and will change every time you apply— customize, customize, customize!

Taking Your Career from Classroom to Cubicle

32

If possible, address your letter to an actual person. If you cannot track down the hiring manager's name, personalize as best you can.

33

While each paragraph in your cover letter will be short, your first should be the shortest.

34

Sentence one of your cover letter: [Succinctly explain why you admire the organization and are choosing to apply.]

35

Sentence two of your cover letter: Please consider me for the [title] position at [company] advertised on [where you saw the job ad].

36

Sentence three of your cover letter: My [quality/skill], [quality/skill], and [degree/major] from [school] make me an ideal candidate.

37

Cover letter paragraphs two and three both will be taken from the cache of accomplishment stories you developed in the last section.

38

Be sure you connect the accomplishment's importance to the position for or organization at which you are applying.

39

In the fourth cover letter paragraph, indicate that you've included all the information requested in the position advertisement.

40

If you are applying outside of your area, be sure to indicate you are extremely interested in relocating and will do so at your expense.

41

Conclude your cover letter with a "call to action": If I don't hear from you beforehand, I will follow up in one week.

Taking Your Career from Classroom to Cubicle

42

End your cover letter by thanking the reader for his or her time and consideration in reviewing your application materials.

43

For your résumé, use the same font, point size, and "letterhead" as your cover letter.

44

Do *not* include an objective statement on your résumé. Instead, include a professional profile.

45

Develop a professional profile by knowing what is required, desired, and valued. Then, think about what makes you fit.

46

Under Education, list your school's name, location, graduation date, degree, major, minor, and GPA if 3.0 or above.

47

Under Experience, do *not* include any experience not *directly* related to the position for which you are applying.

48

What counts as experience? Internships, volunteer work, class projects, leadership roles, and starting your own business.

49

List your position title first (**bolded**), then the organization name (*italicized*). The position is more important than where you held it.

50

Organize the Experience section in reverse chronological order (most recent position first by the date you *began* the position).

51

Under each position, include up to three bullets. Begin each with an action verb. Focus on accomplishments, not just job duties.

52

If you have large gaps in your résumé due to removing all unrelated positions, include them in Additional Experience. No bullets.

53

Under Skills & Accomplishments, include any *related* awards you received, computer programs you know, etc.

54

Do not include a list of your references or "References available upon request" statement at the end of your résumé. This is implied.

55

A presence on Twitter, LinkedIn, Facebook, and Come Recommended will help you connect directly with hiring managers.

Taking Your Career from Classroom to Cubicle

56

Many hiring managers use Twitter as a recruiting tool and have begun tweeting their openings.

57

Choose a Twitter username consistent with your personal brand, customize your page, and complete your bio.

58

Tweets are limited to 140 characters, so choose your words wisely. Also, consider carefully whether or not to abbreviate.

59

Tweet often and be relevant. Share information useful to those following you, such as hiring managers and thought leaders.

60

Stay "on brand" by not letting your personal life show up too often and too strong.

61

Retweet information tweeted by others that you find interesting and so would your followers.

62

To help manage your Twitter experience, download a third-party desktop application.

63

For a great tutorial about getting involved on LinkedIn, visit http://grads.linkedin.com.

64

Facebook can be used in a similar manner to LinkedIn. Check your content, your friends' content, and your privacy settings.

65

Add information from your résumé, post portfolio samples that might catch a hiring manager's eye, and become "fans" of Facebook pages.

66

Facebook also now has custom URLs, so be sure to reserve yours! Again, this should be consistent with your personal brand.

67

To create your profile on Come Recommended, copy and paste from your résumé, upload a picture, and attach portfolio samples.

68

When prompted on Come Recommended, insert your references' email addresses and send your recommendation requests. Three are required.

69

Having an online portfolio is just one more way to get noticed and increase your search rank.

70

Start building an online portfolio. At http://www.whois.com, find out if your personal domain name is for sale (i.e., firstnamelastname.com).

71

Purchase your domain name and hosting at the same time.

72

I recommend building and designing your online portfolio using a free content management system such as WordPress.

73

On the homepage of your online portfolio, include a welcome message to visitors—this can be similar to your cover letter.

74

Create a page on your portfolio where visitors can download your résumé in PDF format. iPaper is a good application.

75

Create a page on your portfolio for your *actual* portfolio—samples of your previous work that would be of interest to hiring managers.

76

If you have a professional blog, link to it from your online portfolio. If you don't, think about creating one.

77

Finally, create a tab on your portfolio with your contact information or a form through which hiring managers can contact you.

78

Be sure to include the link to your online portfolio in your cover letter and on your résumé.

79

Because you never know when you might run into a potential employer, invest in a set of business cards.

80

On the front of your business card, include your name, major, phone number, e-mail address, and link to your online portfolio.

81

On the back of your business card, include a version of your professional profile from your résumé.

82

When employers ask you for references, 99 percent of the time they will actually call them. So, be prepared.

83

References can be current or previous employers, industry professionals, professors/teachers, and other non-family members.

84

Ask your intended references if they would be willing to serve as your reference.

85

Ask your intended references what they would say about you if called by a hiring manager. You don't want surprises!

Taking Your Career from Classroom to Cubicle

Section III

Networking as a Job Search Tool

Unfortunately, despite the fact that an estimated 80 percent of jobs are secured through networking, it is not taught at most colleges and universities. In this chapter, you will learn the ins and outs of networking online and offline.

86

The overall goal of networking is to create a two-way, mutually beneficial relationship—and it's important to landing a job.

87

Another important networking rule to remember is: build a relationship first and ask for favors second.

88

Networking rules online are fairly straightforward: listen, be relevant, mind your brand, engage, and give more than get.

89

When you attend a networking event, what do you bring with you? Business cards? Your full résumé? A copy of your portfolio?

90

One networking tool you need but might be leaving at home is your 60-second story—who are you and what are you seeking?

91

If you can't grab someone's attention within a matter of seconds at a networking event, his/her mind has already wandered.

92

If you're a nervous networker, you might want to write out your 60-second story and practice it in front of a mirror.

93

But, be careful not to over-practice your "elevator pitch"—you don't want to sound rehearsed!

94

Most of all, be honest. If you start off the networking relationship being dishonest, it won't get very far.

95

So, bring a set of business cards to your next networking event, but leave everything else at home except your story.

96

Be prepared to listen to other people's stories. Make a mental list of how you can help them in exchange for them helping you.

97

Don't just hand out as many business cards as possible. Instead, engage in a handful of meaningful conversations.

98

On the back of other people's business cards, make notes about them and your conversation.

99

When you get home, invite them to connect with you on LinkedIn so you can keep track of their contact information even if they change jobs.

Taking Your Career from Classroom to Cubicle

100

Reach out once a month: ask how work is going, invite him/her out to coffee, share an interesting article, etc.

101

When you finally ask for help, politely explain your situation, be respectful of the individual's time, and say thank you.

102

Don't forget to offer networking contacts help in return—preferably even before you ask for assistance.

Taking Your Career from Classroom to Cubicle

Section IV

Applying for Internships & Entry-Level Jobs

As a young professional, you likely don't have much experience applying for jobs. This chapter will take you through the hiring process from start to finish.

103

The hardest part—preparing your career tools—is already done! They will be on the frontlines of your entry-level job search.

104

If you didn't have much internship experience during college, I recommend applying for internships upon graduation.

105

The definition of entry-level is changing, and many companies now require two years' experience.

Taking Your Career from Classroom to Cubicle

106

Learn new interviewing technologies. If employers are using them, you need to too.

107

Clean up your online image. First impressions count, and, yes, employers are watching.

108

Create a written job search plan.

109

Set weekly goals. All goals included in your plan should indicate specific actions you will take by certain dates.

110

Target specific organizations—your focus should be on *quality* not quantity.

111

Take careful notes. Under each organization, include bullet points from your research that will be important to remember.

112

Read industry publications and blogs. It's important to keep up with the news and latest trends in your industry.

113

Arrange informational interviews to allow you to better understand an organization's culture and the industry itself.

114

Attend at least one networking event each week. It's important to step away from your computer and get out of the house.

115

While they are often massive and difficult to determine what's a real job and what isn't, don't dismiss job boards entirely.

Taking Your Career from Classroom to Cubicle

116

If you say you're going to do something, do it. If you make a new networking contact, arrange to have coffee with them.

117

Read the job ads very carefully and follow all the instructions.

118

Follow up after every stage of the hiring process—typically every seven to ten days.

119

Be willing to volunteer if you don't land a job immediately.

Taking Your Career from Classroom to Cubicle

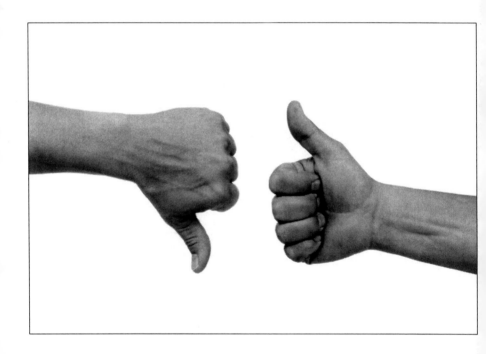

Section V

Accepting & Rejecting Offers

There is an expected etiquette when either accepting or rejecting an offer. Again, because this is an area in which young professionals are extremely inexperienced, this chapter will outline the rules for you.

120

If you don't want to burn bridges, it's wise to follow the etiquette for accepting and rejecting job offers.

121

When you receive an offer, tell the employer you are honored, excited, and will get back to him/her within the next 24 hours.

122

Be sure to get any job offer in writing before you officially accept.

123

A phone call, followed by an email or signed documents, is the proper protocol for accepting a job offer.

124

A hiring manager who offers you a job likely knows other employers looking to hire.

125

When rejecting an offer, call. Politely but firmly say, "I appreciate the offer, but I've decided not to accept."

126

State that you did not come by this decision lightly and mention a couple of specific reasons for saying "no" if pressed.

Taking Your Career from Classroom to Cubicle

Section VI

Succeeding on the Job

It's not enough to have a job; you have to succeed right from the beginning so you're not the last one in and the first one out. This chapter will briefly describe how to win over your boss and colleagues right from the start.

127

Make a powerful first impression. On the first day, show you are ready to work by walking in on time and exuding a can-do attitude.

128

Always show up to your job appropriately dressed and well-groomed.

129

Over-deliver on your first assignment. If your boss asks for three examples, give five.

130

Never leave your office or cube without a notebook and pen, PDA, laptop, or other note-taking device.

131

If you are not entirely certain you understand what your supervisor wants when he or she has given you an assignment, speak up!

132

Become the go-to person for something in the office, whether it's building PowerPoint presentations or navigating social media.

Taking Your Career from Classroom to Cubicle

133

Keep your opinions to yourself, and be aware of negative "types" in the office. Don't partake in gossip!

134

Learn people's names and roles in the organization quickly.

135

Be observant about your supervisor's communication preferences.

136

Your boss comes first, even if other key employees request support.

137

Express a positive attitude and a lot of interest in your new position.

138

Take initiative. Be the first one to volunteer to take on new projects, and don't wait for assignments to come to you.

139

Find a mentor. Connect with someone, not necessarily in your department, that you can go to for advice.

140

Mind your manners. Always say "please" and "thank you," even if others don't.

About the Author

Heather R. Huhman, Founder and President of Come Recommended, is passionate about helping students and recent college graduates pursue their dream careers. As the oldest child in her family—even among her extended family—she did not have anyone to guide her through the trials and tribulations of developing her career. Now, as an experienced hiring manager and someone who has been in nearly every employment-related situation imaginable, she is serving as that much-needed guide for others.

Heather knows and understands the needs of today's employers and internship and entry-level job seekers. Her expertise in this area led to her selection as Examiner.

com's entry-level careers columnist in mid-2008. The daily, national column educates high school students through recent college graduates about how to find, land, and succeed at internships and entry-level jobs.

Additionally, Heather is a career expert for the CAREEREALISM Twitter Advice Project, the job search expert for Campus Calm, a contributor to One Day, One Job, One Day, One Internship, and Personal Branding Blog and author of the e-books 'Relocating for an Entry-Level Job: Why You Probably Have to & How to Do It' and 'Gen Y Meets the Workforce: Launching Your Career During Economic Uncertainty.'

Heather resides in the Washington, D.C. area with her husband, dog, and two cats.

LaVergne, TN USA
01 February 2010
171651LV00001B/2/P